LETTERS
OF FAITH

LETTERS OF FAITH

DAVID DOUGLAS

INTRODUCTION

I remember. . .

I had gone to West Virginia to battle poverty and the mining that tore open mountains for coal. I came looking for changes that I could work, saving hills and people in picturesque danger.

I was unprepared for the change that would be worked in me.

I had arrived in Appalachia one September disbelieving in Jesus, and I left a year later no longer disbelieving.

What difference has that belief made in my life since then?

After more than forty years, it is time to write openly of the difference.

And to answer the question Jesus asked of his disciples, *"Who do you say that I am?"*

And to remember how belief in Jesus came about in West Virginia.

I had not originally planned to work with churches. I was twenty-two years old, a recent college graduate. For one year before entering law school, I envisioned working in a poor section of the country. I could have easily have volunteered, and nearly did, with a federal poverty program instead. It was the social—not religious—witness of Christian churches in Appalachia that drew me: food pantries and clothing stores for the poor, networks to care for the sick, protests (at least by some residents) against strip-mining of mountains and pollution of creeks.

As a religion major in college I had taken classes to tell me of all the world's faiths, except Christianity. I opened no New Testament chapters on my way to a degree. In retrospect, I realized that the religion department's professors bent rules to let me graduate.

A pastor in West Virginia who knew one of my professors called me the spring before graduation. He heard I was interested in working in rural Appalachia. Three churches along Coal River in Raleigh County could employ me to work with their youth groups. Was I interested? Churches had deeper roots than did government agencies in the Appalachian communities, he said.

I told him I wasn't a Christian. I said I believed in God who had created the world, and I had studied the Old Testament, particularly the prophets. But I saw no need for Jesus. I gave the pastor reasons why I disbelieved. I briefly inveighed against Jesus like the lawyer I would soon become, listing my objections at a rapid, heated pace like a man after too many cups of coffee. "Jesus was unnecessary. . . Jesus couldn't have been who he said he was. . .Christians excluded others . . . Christians were hypocrites. . ."

He listened. He replied that there were others who could provide spiritual leadership for the youth groups. But could I, he asked, drive a VW van with a bad clutch?

And so I would come to spend a year in the heart of West Virginia, employed by three churches to lead their youth groups. I felt like an illiterate hired to be a librarian.

The churches paid me a few dollars a week and arranged room and board with obliging families in the congregations. A quarterly check from home supplemented me, like a raft that allowed me to float above their poverty.

Each of us finds a place where clarity begins. Where, more than any other setting, we listen as though for the first time. A Quaker once wrote of believing "that Jesus could be known now as truly as he was known by the disciples." If that speaks of a crossing a line of recognition, I felt I crossed it in West Virginia.

No Damascus Road conversion, no lightning bolt of sudden insight, convinced me. Rather a slow process of scattered incidents and snatches of conversations, some recounted in the following pages, drew me imperceptibly past obstacles and toward Jesus. They might not have persuaded others. But at that time in my life, in that place, they were collectively enough for me.

In those mountains a difference of inches caused rain falling on a ridge to run into two different rivers. I arrived one September to one side of a ridge of disbelief. By shifting only slightly, I found when I left a year later that I had crossed over into a watershed of faith.

I left West Virginia more than four decades ago.

Jesus once asked the disciples: *"Who do you say that I am?"* My own answer comes from what the Bible reveals and orthodox creeds confirm, and from what I have experienced first-hand these past decades.

I have been struck by the spectrum of actions that Jesus takes in our lives. Jesus. . . 'comforts,' 'forgives,' 'demands we repent,' 'loves,' 'bears our sins,' 'rescues,' 'warns'. . .

As I made a list of such words, most of them verbs and all of them anchored in scripture, I began to fashion them into an alphabet from A to Z. A mnemonic way to remind myself how I would answer his question,*"Who do you say that I am?"*

There are of course more actions that those represented by twenty six letters of the alphabet. St. John ended his Gospel by noting that all the world's books could not contain what Jesus does. Another person might choose an entirely different set of words to describe what Jesus does in one's life.

But these twenty-six actions describe what Jesus does my life and in the lives of many down through history. Each time I walk through this alphabet of faith I find fresh examples of each word coming to mind.

A close friend once asked me with some insistence, "But what difference does it make to you to believe?" In the pages that follow I imagine it is Jesus who asks that very question: *"What difference does it make?"*

I have denied Jesus in different ways over the years, now most often by failing to remember. Not that I forget; rather I do not take time to remember. These words from A to Z are ways for me to take time to remember.

Time is short. What I choose to emphasize today might change in another year. But we are not given the certainty of more years. So these pages are as true as I can make them now. Each entry is written, as in a prayer, to Jesus.

I remember. . .

LETTERS
OF FAITH

A is for ABBA

"Who do you say that I am?"

You spoke of God as *"Abba, Father."*

"Abba, Father, all things are possible to thee; remove this cup from me; yet not what I will, but what thou wilt." (Mark 14:36)

"Abba." The word that means 'Papa' or 'Daddy' in Aramaic. The word that children in the Middle East still use for their own fathers.

Does any single word in Scripture disclose more who you were?

I remember. . . an elderly woman living beside Coal River with her husband, a retired miner. As part of my meager compensation, members of the churches offered meals, and I would join this couple once a week for dinner. As she prayed, she would sit with eyes closed and sunken shoulders, ancient bones with their marrow of faith.

Others might pray to someone rumored; she prayed to someone known. As she offered a blessing for the food, it was not a rote prayer that I was accustomed to. She said "Father" with a sense of intimacy and proximity that startled me.

I had envisioned God as thunderously remote. Awe, dependence and distance—all this I had tremblingly felt before. Her praying introduced a closeness to God I had not considered.

"What difference does it make?"

You not only spoke the word "Abba" but invited your followers to adopt it as well. As St. Paul wrote: *"Because we are his children, God has sent the Spirit of his Son into our hearts, crying 'Abba, Father."* (Galatians 4:6)

If I had traveled all the world's sacred paths and asked all the spiritual leaders, who else would have invited me to address the God of Creation as "Abba"?

"It is we who give God other titles—'High and Mighty,' 'King of Kings,' 'Lord of "Lords,' noted J.B. Phillips. "These are fine-sounding words, but they obscure the real nature of God and his true relationship with us."

That intimacy is not something to take for granted. I should not presume too much. *"For as the heavens are higher than the earth, so are my ways higher than your ways and my thoughts than your thoughts."* (Isaiah 55:9)

But when my faith grows inattentive, speaking the word "Abba" can be enough to convert my wandering mind into prayerful conversation.

Does any single word in Scripture disclose more who we are?

B is for BEAR OUR SINS

"Who do you say that I am?"

You bear our sins.

"Jesus himself bore our sins in his body on the cross, so that we might die to sin and live to righteousness." (1st Peter 2:24)

"Jesus Himself is the expiation for our sins; and not for ours only, but also for those of the whole world." (1st John 2:2)

"God loved us and sent His Son to be the propitiation for our sins." (1st John 4:10)

I remember. . . attending church each Sunday with the family who housed me that autumn. I had seen living rooms larger than the sanctuary: a narrow aisle flanked on either side by 10 rows of uncushioned pews led down to a plain wooden table. At the time of announcements, I would stand and sketch the youth groups' activities for the upcoming week. No one questioned my credentials.

I felt like someone hired to be a lifeguard while wearing a suit of armor. The hour-long worship services seemed unending. I sensed the incongruity of my presence. I was a so-called "flatlander" in Appalachian hills, and a disbeliever in Christ in a Christian pew. At first I treated the worship services like a sociological journey into a foreign culture.

When the congregation sang hymns, I winced at the stanzas' sentimentality: *"Jesus paid it all/ All to Him I owe/ Sin had left a crimson stain/ He washed it white as snow. . ."*

But imperceptibly during the year, as the congregation began "Rock of Ages" or "In the Garden," I found myself beginning to sway discretely in time to the music, joining in the singing before understanding the lyrics.

"What difference does it make?"

I know there was purpose in what you did on the cross.

Lifting, unburdening, removing from us a weight of sin, guilt, misdeed, vice—whatever we call it—and shifting the burden to yourself.

Others try to describe this in various ways: "There was a transference of sin from sinners to Christ. . . his own self bore that sin." "The Doctor suffered the cost and the sick received the healing." "He came to pay a debt he didn't owe because we owed a debt we couldn't pay."

We can deny the burden exists, or that we need help lifting it. And over time, left to ourselves, that weight pressing down grows intolerable.

No one else has claimed to bear our sin, much less to have actually done it. Is there a more shining act in history?

I too often forget that its purpose includes even me. Then memory returns and the only words to say are, "Thank you."

C is for COMFORT

"Who do you say that I am?"

You comfort us.

"For as we share abundantly in Christ's sufferings, so through Christ we share abundantly in comfort too." (2 Corinthians 1:5)

"I can do all things through Christ who strengthens me." (Philippians 4:13)

"Peace I leave with you. My peace I give to you; not as the world gives do I give to you. Let not your heart be troubled, neither let it be afraid." (John 14:27)

I remember. . . a woman who returned home from the hospital, the doctor acceding to her wish. Her pancreatic cancer gave her little time. Neighbors arranged round-the-clock nursing care. When I visited she spoke to me about her parent's life in a coal camp and their winter diet of roots and potatoes. She talked about the cancer's pain. Drugs provided only a thin membrane of relief; pain soon squeezed through. It was how she was dying, not death itself, that grieved her. She spoke of wanting "to be with Jesus." Verses she'd known since childhood strengthened her: *"In my Father's house are many rooms. . . I go to prepare a place for you. . .Come unto me all you who labor and are heavy laden and I will give you rest."* Words of solace, like beams of a coal mine, that buttressed in the dark.

And I remember as well a pastor who weathered slander and ostracism as he condemned strip-mining's poisoned streams and ravaged hilltops. Comparing strip-mining to "temple desecration," he excoriated "crimes against creation," angering owners of coal companies and miners across the state, some in his own parish. Complaints and late night telephone calls showered down on him. Neighbors forbad their children to play with his. Newspapers eventually headlined his ouster. It was one thing to speak out here, another to be vilified, and I doubt I would have risked either from a pulpit. The pastor's protest undercut any image of ministers as equivocating, tremulous souls. Elsewhere Christianity might be indicted as a tranquilizer. Here I encountered it more as a detonator.

"What difference does it make?"

"Comfort" means not only solace but fortitude, as in the word's original dual sense. Both a shawl for the shoulders and steel for the spine.

Where does it originate? Not from within ourselves, but from you.

It comes when I hold on to your cross, contending with what could otherwise overwhelm—sickness, fear, anxiety, loneliness, despair.

In every season of our lives, it comes as your gift. That we might also extend it to others.

I rely daily on your comfort in all its fullness.

D is for DEMAND

"Who do you say that I am?"

You demand we repent.

"For I am not come to call the righteous, but sinners to repentance." (Luke 5:32)

"Repent, for the kingdom of heaven is at hand." (Matthew 4:17)

"For all have sinned and fall short of the glory of God." (Romans 3:23)

I remember. . . a retired coal miner in Montcoal. I sat in his kitchen as he eased his body into a worn wooden rocker. High blood pressure reddened his bulbous nose and ears. His outsized, florid features gave him an unsightly expression at first. But he had kindly eyes and a smile that bisected his face from ear to mammoth ear. He told me he had once been at a tent revival meeting near Charleston, drunk for days, listening to a preacher, a former miner himself, whose drinking led him to mistreat others. The preacher told a story: a slatefall injured him once and he was taken to the hospital in Charleston where he promised God he'd change his life if he got well. He carved his initials into the wooden bedframe over his head to pass the time. He recovered, soon forgot his promise and went back to drinking. Another mine accident sent him to the hospital. Flat on his back, he looked up and saw he was in the same bed, with his initials staring down at him. He recovered, "backslid" again, and for a third time, a mine injury took him to the hospital. This time he awoke on a different floor, but when he looked up at the bedframe, there were his initials. The promise came back and this time it took.

The miner looked at me and said that night when the preacher asked people "to come to the altar to accept Christ," he got up and went. He had not taken a drink since.

On some Sunday mornings in the church at Montcoal, the congregation would sing stanzas from the miner's favorite hymn: *"I was sinking deep in sin, Far from the peaceful shore. . . Love lifted me, Love lifted me. . .When nothing else could help, Love lifted me."*

As he boomed lyrics off-key, from the bottom of his battered heart, I knew his singing expressed no second -hand conviction.

"What difference does it make?"

Repentance was not an overused word in my vocabulary at the age twenty-two. It signaled medicine needed for the ill and I felt well. Repent? Of what? And now it seems a response always in season. As congregations confess to you in unison: "We *have left undone those things which we ought to have done; and we have done those things which we ought not to have done."*

We are not as well as we wish. You welcome us as patients to a hospital, the only requirement for admission being our admission of infirmity. Malcolm Muggeridge wrote, "It is precisely when you consider the best in man that you see there is in each of us a hard core pride or self-centeredness which corrupts our best achievements and blights our best experiences."

One of the first words of your ministry was *"Repent."* I start each day from where I hope not to end.

E is for EMBARRASS

"Who do you say that I am?"

You embarrass us.

"For whoever is ashamed of me and of my words, of them will the Son of man be ashamed when he comes in his glory and in the glory of the Father and of the holy angles." (Luke 9:26)

"But again Peter denied with an oath that he had been with Jesus of Nazareth: 'I do not know the man.'" (Matthew 26:72)

"Because, if you confess with your mouth that Jesus is Lord and believe in your heart that God raised him from the dead, you will be saved." (Romans 10:9)

I remember. . . the Appalachian men and women, often broken in some way, who had faith slant through them like beams of light. Plain spoken people, they told the Christian story simply without diluting it. Employed by churches, I was expected to call on families of the youth groups, and parents who believed faith had changed their lives spoke about it without hesitation. I winced at first to hear them talk so unguardedly. But looking back on the year in West Virginia, who would I like most to encounter again? Those whose witness made me the most uncomfortable.

"What difference does it make?"

For years, when asked about my time in West Virginia, I would mention teenagers in the youth group or students in the high school or ministers who protested the strip-mining of mountains.

Everyone, in other words, but you.

I did not want to witness. To say that "It was there I came to believe in Jesus" (groping for words imprecise but authentic) might distance me from others. I omitted your name rather than risk sinking in others' esteem.

"For they loved human praise more than the praise of God." (John 12:43).

We do well to be ashamed of our timidity. Your warning is clear, potentially lifesaving: *"Whoever acknowledges me before others, I will also acknowledge him before my Father in heaven; but whoever disowns me before others, I will disown before my Father in heaven."* (Matthew 10:32-33)

In seeking to be known by those who will forget us, we avoid acknowledging the one who will always remember us.

F is for FORGIVE

"Who do you say that I am?"

You forgive us.

"Neither do I condemn you . . . go and sin no more." (John 8:11)

"The Son of man has authority on earth to forgive sins." (Matthew 9:6)

"Your sins are forgiven." (Luke 7:48)

I remember. . . a pastor describing Coal River's parishioners this way: "Deep down, they're all asking the same question: *'Am I really forgiven?'*" The pastor would remind them of divine forgiveness, often through the story of the prodigal son who left home, departed to a far country, squandered everything then, contrite, set out toward home expecting a rebuke only to be met by his father rushing to meet him. Each Sunday morning service, the pastor would utter familiar words: "The good news is that, in Jesus Christ, we are forgiven. Let us now forgive one another." But more than a few parishioners stoked grievances. With names like Hatfield and McCoy (the youth group included both clans) families could guard grudges like heirlooms.

The pastor told me of two brothers who lived next door to each other far up Dry Creek. They had not spoken to each other for twenty years, angered by some distant dispute. Even as the older brother lay dying at home, the younger one refused to cross the chasm of a backyard. The pastor did not give up. He continued to visit both brothers, concentrating his plea on the younger. "You can go to him; he can't walk. You need to take the first step." Week after week, the pastor cobbled together a bridge by perseverance and prayer.The younger brother finally relented and with the pastor beside him crossed the backyard as though it were mined. He entered the house for the first time in decades and hesitantly moved toward the bed. There was silence, and then he said simply, "I'm sorry." Through tears his older brother raised a hand that was grasped by his sibling.

In the land of the Hatfields and McCoys, a deadlock was broken on a deathbed.

"What difference does it make?"

Each passing year I come to know more deeply my own need to be forgiven.

You forgive, if we approach asking for forgiveness. I have sensed this happening to me while understanding it only imperfectly.

What seems discomfortingly clear is that forgiveness can be contingent: *"Forgive us our sins as we forgive those who sin against us."*

Yet because you forgive, so can we, making possible journeys we could not undertake otherwise.

G is for GAVE

"Who do you say that I am?"

You gave your life for us.

"For the Son of man also came not to be served but to serve, and to give his life as a ransom for many." (Mark 10:45)

"I lay down my life of my own accord." (John 10:18)

"I live by faith in the Son of God who loved me and gave himself for me." (Galatians 2:20)

I remember. . . when I first came to West Virginia I ignored the crucifixion. When I saw depictions of the man on a cross, I averted my eyes as though from a highway accident. As long as I did not see, I need not respond. It was a story for others, not a sacrifice for me.

At the age of twenty two, I did not want to be beholden to anyone. I preferred to say, "I have accomplished things on my own." No wonder I denied the claim of a life given for my benefit. If I acknowledged that act, what obligations might ensue?

But I could turn away for only so long. Stories of sacrifice veined these mountains. People elsewhere could dismiss as a figure of speech the words, *"Greater love has no man than this, that a man lay down his life for his friends."* For some miners in Appalachia, however, the words were not a metaphor but their epitaph.

The story that one man had sacrificed his life for all people took years to grow in me, but the seed was watered along Coal River.

"What difference does it make?"

Long after leaving West Virginia, I visited a quiet cathedral for prayer. I sat there in a pew and looked up at the crucifix.

At last I'd grasped what Coal River's hymns and sermons had been proclaiming. I had viewed crucifixes impassively before, mindful more of the art than the underlying act. For the first time, the cross of thorns seemed to scrape the head, the cross bar wrench the arms, the nails savage the hands and feet. I imagined how it must have felt to die this way, pierced, immobilized, ridiculed.

The sermons and Scriptural passages that described the sacrifice—all their once-leaden words changed into light.

In a sudden burst of understanding, I exclaimed silently to myself, "You did <u>that</u>, for me?" (Just then another visitor to the sanctuary happened into my line of sight, and I amended my question: "You did <u>that</u>, for <u>us</u>?")

Still startled, in a daze of gratitude, I inhaled deeply and asked, "What can I do for you?"

H is for HEAL

"Who do you say that I am?"

You heal.

"And he healed many who were sick with various diseases." (Mark 1:34)

"And he went throughout all Galilee . . . healing every disease and every affliction among the people." (Matthew 4:23)

"And many followed him, and he healed them all . . ." (Matthew 12:15)

I remember. . . a play about Holy Week performed in the rural churches by the combined youth groups. As leader, I'd expected merely to direct the production, but an additional role that no teenager wanted came my way: by default, I portrayed Judas.

Evening after evening in the Appalachian twilight, with church windows wide, the play rehearsals pieced together the Gospel story for me. Until then I'd really known only portions of it—scattered sentences and random images like shards of stained glass. Now, hovering at the margins of the play as Judas, I probed the central character with queries not all that unfamiliar to me.

I had known the young actor portraying Jesus only a short time before the play drew him into the youth group. He had shown me his sketches of wildlife, displaying an artistic bent that perplexed his family of coal miners. Now his skill on stage came to the forefront.

As the practices progressed, I saw in his performance, particularly in quiet scenes of healing of lepers and a blind man, a surpassing attentiveness and compassion.

In the evenings when I read a Scriptural account of healing, I would envision the actor's face as he stretched out his hand to those seeking to be healed.

In my role as Judas, I watched from the shadows as scenes from a play put into limelight the reality of healing.

"What difference does it make?"

You heal us. Not necessarily by our deadlines or in expected ways. But healing occurs. The miracles you chose to work, as Frank Sheed pointed out, "were those which would bring relief to suffering, solace to anguish."

At times I have held on to the cross as though clutching a ship's mast in a storm, as I waited for healing to occur.

I continue to pray daily for healing, or some aspect of it, for others or for myself. A restoration, like a spring of water, to wash wounds that are physical, psychological, and spiritual.

I take nothing for granted. But I know that in your time, in your way, healing will take place.

I is for INCLUDE

"Who do you say that I am?"

You include everyone.

"If a man has a hundred sheep, and one of them has gone astray, does he not leave the ninety-nine on the mountains and go in search of the one that went astray?" (Matthew 18:12)

"For God so loved the world. . ." (John 3:16)

I remember. . . the congregations in Coal River churches: the whiskey-scented grandmother flanked by the fastidious school librarian; the crippled miner sitting across from the well-dressed coal company superintendent; two misshapen brothers slow of thought sharing a pew with a retired coal-company physicist. A friend of mine elsewhere, years earlier, had once complained to me, "Christianity feels like a party I haven't been invited to." I myself had once considered Christianity like a fortress with a slender drawbridge and strict admission requirements. But casting an eye over those eclectic West Virginian pews, I began to reconsider the absence of an invitation.

That autumn I talked with the crippled miner at his small kitchen table. I told him about a college acquaintance who wore religion on his sleeve and once insisted, "Jesus said that no one comes to God except through knowing Jesus."

I challenged the miner: "How could that claim be so? I believe in God. I already pray to God. I don't need Jesus."

I objected not only on my behalf, but those in history who would never have heard Jesus' name. What about them, how could they be excluded?

The miner listened as I spoke. He nodded his long, worn face, watching me with merry eyes, smiling not in condescension but as though for some reason he cared very much for me. As I berated Christianity's exclusivity, he poured us more coffee and turned his good ear to hear me better.

"What difference does it make?"

My initial objection of unfairness—that people who had never heard of you were somehow excluded from divine favor—would be undone by a simple insight from C.S. Lewis: "We do know that no man can be saved except through Christ. We do not know that only those who <u>know</u> Him can be saved through Him."

I had confused human cognition with divine mercy.

Ironically, I'd been so sure Christians excluded others that I'd neglected how I did so myself. Employed by Coal River churches, my job prompted me to enter sick rooms and rotting homes—often housing personalities I would not have sought out on my own. When I left the valley's incubation, I wondered, would I draw lines, glancing indifferently or contemptuously at others? Or would deepening faith nudge me into corners of the world I would otherwise neglect? And once there, looking at strangers I might have ignored, not draw lines but cross them?

It is a question I answered not once for all time but each day.

J is for JUDGE

"Who do you say that I am?"

You judge us.

"The Father judges no one, but has given all judgment to the Son. . ." (John 5:22)

"For we shall all stand before the judgment seat of Christ." (Romans 14:10)

I remember. . . several teenagers asking me to drive them to hear a renowned itinerant preacher at a Rock Creek church. A tall, white-haired, distinguished man of sixty, he started his sermon conversationally, smiling broadly, his coal-black eyes alert behind wire rim glasses. I strained to hear him at first. Then, pacing the floor as pinewood planks rumbled under his feet, he began to castigate unnamed sinners. His voice began to move faster, erratically, like a boulder rolling downhill, and he built up enormous speed before leaving his listeners exhausted at the end of an hour.

He led the congregation in singing hymns about winding up on the right side of the river of life.

When the trumpet of the Lord shall sound/
    And time shall be no more
And the morning breaks eternal bright and fair
When the saved diverse shall gather/ Over on the other shore
And the roll is call up yonder, I'll be there

And as he sang the stanzas I thought: Really? How can he be so sure?

I was more taken by another minister's rueful admission later that year: "It's a shame I don't practice what I preach, but it would be a disaster if I preached what I practiced."

"What difference does it make?"

I am uncomfortable being in your line of sight. I prefer to think of others needing to be judged. But that evasion doesn't work long. *"But who are you that you judge your neighbor?"* (James 4:12)

I know actions have consequences; a reckoning must come. I do not know the verdict, but I can surely hope for clemency. I find some consolation in that 'judging' is not the ultimate point: *"For God sent the Son into the world, not to condemn the world, but that the world might be saved through him."* (John 3:17)

At times, the only thing to do is to join my voice to the well-worn prayer of others down the centuries: "Lord Jesus Christ, Son of God, have mercy on me, a sinner."

K is for KNOW

"Who do you say that I am?"

You know us by name.

"O Lord, you have searched me and known me. You know when I sit down and when I rise up; you discern my thoughts from afar. You search out my path and my lying down and are acquainted with all my ways."(Psalm 139:1-3)

"Are not two sparrows sold for a penny? And not one of them will fall to the ground without your Father's will. But even the hairs of your head are all numbered." (Matthew 10:29-30)

"For we are his workmanship, created in Christ Jesus for good works, which God prepared beforehand that we should walk in them." (Ephesians 2:10)

I remember. . . the mother who kept her kitchen open all day, with a welcoming fire, where anyone in the valley could find pinto beans, boiled cabbage, corn bread, apple crisp and coffee. A large, cheerful woman, her face flushed crimson as she ladled beans from an ancient stove. She considered this work her calling. Gathered at her kitchen table she saw not the valley's "poor" but each distinct person.

Sermons along the Coal River had insisted that "God leaves no one uncounted.". . ."From the one lost sheep to the prodigal son, each person is visible to God."

Appalachia did not teach me that I was known by name. I don't think I ever doubted that. What I began to sense here, unsettling my narcissistic heart, was that each of us is known by name.

"What difference does it make?"

If you know each of us by name, then no one is invisible, no one counts for nothing. We are reminded not only who we are but whose we are. As one writer notes: "Our own experience of the Lord is likely to be one of 'being known' as much as 'knowing.'"

When Mother Teresa comforted the sick and dying in Calcutta she didn't respond to the collective poor but because she saw "Jesus in distressing disguise" in each distinct person.

In the last light of day, all our memberships will expire, and we are left alone belonging to the one who has known our name from the beginning.

May we come to see each other as you see us.

L is for LOVE

"Who do you say that I am?"

You love us.

"As I have loved you, so you are to love one another."
(John 13:34)

"Love one another as I have loved you." (John 15:12)

I remember. . . arriving in West Virginia in the rain, driving on narrow roads past homes perched in fog on the sides of steep hills. A family had offered to house me my first month in the valley, and I parked my car on the incline, running toward the house through rain while clutching my suitcase and guitar. The middle-aged widow with three sons opened the screen door wide to greet me. She burst into laughter when she saw how I towered over her.

In those first days I would offer to help with breakfast in the kitchen. She would have none of it, ordering me to sit down in front of enormous breakfasts of eggs, cornbread and potatoes. She stood across the kitchen table from me, breathing heavily from the exertion, watching me eat. Her pancreatic cancer had spread and doctors gave her less than six months to live.

I imposed on her family only that first month before taking up a neighboring family's offer to house me. But from the moment I entered through her screen door, I felt a sense of unconditional welcome. "Soon as I heard you were coming, I wanted to be the first to give you a place to stay," she had said. Whatever my shortcomings were, they were set aside in her eyes. Despite her frail health, her preoccupation with three sons about to be orphans, she cared for me my first month in the valley as if I was the one who was dying.

"What difference does it make?"

I knew of your love more by hearsay and viewed it as a metaphor.

But when I first felt it, the experience lasted only briefly, like a moment of grace suspended above doubt before gravity reconvened. It stirred no ecstatic shout but rather joy and a quiet murmur, "So this is what it's all about." It came as an encompassing, luminous sense of love that extinguished questions and could not be forgotten.

We love because you first loved us. "The most wonderful part of the gospel message is that God loves us unconditionally," wrote Brother Roger of Taize.

I read your twin command, *"You shall love the Lord your God with all your heart, and with all your soul, and with all your mind,"* and *"You shall love your neighbor as yourself."* (Matthew 22:37, 39)

Love of God and love of neighbor seem like longitude and latitude for locating the fabled purpose of life. At their intersection is where I hope to live.

M is for MAKE KNOWN

"Who do you say that I am?"

You make God more fully known to us.

"No one has ever seen God; but God's only Son, he who is nearest to the Father's heart, he has made him known." (John 1:18)

"He who has seen me has seen the Father." (John 14:9)

"This is my beloved Son, listen to Him." (Mark 9:7)

I remember. . . the church volunteers at the used clothing store. I assisted them by unpacking enormous cardboard boxes dispatched from more affluent congregations around the country. Boxes offered not only sweaters and gloves but an occasional sequined dress or frayed tuxedo. Large crowds thronged the store's rooms in late autumn, lured by the throat-clearing cough of winter. Some residents rejected the charity, but most didn't, and they paid a nominal sum for cast-off clothing to warm them until spring.

As I prepared to leave one morning, another volunteer noticed I lacked a coat, and reached into one of the boxes to find one for me. I hesitated as he handed it to me. I didn't want it. I already owned coat, though one less warm. More to the point, I had come to the valley to give, not receive. Not wanting to admit I lacked anything I took it only with extreme reluctance.

When I arrived in West Virginia, I denied that I needed anyone to make God more fully known to me. Part of the Christian story reveals what we cannot learn by ourselves alone out under the stars. How was I to accept my need for that grace if I was nearly too close-fisted to accept even a used coat?

"What difference does it make?"

I pay attention to your words and life.

I had known of God through creation. *"Ever since the creation of the world his invisible nature, namely, his eternal power and deity, has been clearly perceived in the things that have been made."* (Romans 1:20)

I had known of God through prophets. *"God, who at various times and in different ways spoke in time past to the fathers by the prophets. . ."* (Hebrews 1:1)

But "Jesus makes known what we would never discover on our own," one writer noted. "Without Jesus we would never know the fullness of God. We would know him as Creator and Designer of all things but we would never know the depth of his compassion toward sinners. . .How fitting that Jesus should be called 'the Word' for he communicates the very nature of God to us."

I have come to know God most clearly through you.

N is for NO

"Who do you say that I am?"

You say, "No. . . do not go that way. . ."

"Enter by the narrow gate. For the gate is wide and the way is easy that leads to destruction, and those who enter by it are many." (Matthew 7:13)

"Every one who hears these words of mine and does not do them will be like a foolish man who built his house upon the sand; and the rain fell, and the floods came and the winds blew and beat against the house, and it fell; and great was the fall of it." (Matthew 7:26)

I remember. . . the coal mine deep inside Montcoal Mountain. I entered its portals once in winter. The mine's foreman, father of a boy in the youth group, had invited me to accompany him underground to see mining operations few visitors ever glimpsed.

Shortly after midnight, he shepherded me into a shuttle car that ran on tracks through the warren of tunnels. With the ceiling inches above my head we leaned over as we hurtled through the dimly-lit tunnels. The foreman kept reminding me, "Don't lift your head." Our shuttle car speed for miles under the low ceiling, and at one point I simply forgot his instruction. As I straightened up, the ceiling immediately nearly ripped the hardhat from my head. My neck was yanked backwards with a terrifying wrench and was sore for weeks thereafter.

We emerged at 4 am from the mouth of the mine. Over-head, winter constellations blazed. Far below in the valley a few kitchen windows seemed to glow with warmth along the river. I had rarely appreciated the lights of either more as I breathed deeply, suspended between homes and stars.

"What difference does it make?"

I believe your stern, sobering guidance. I trust that your "No" is conveyed by one who wants the best for us. Straightforward as advice from the coal mine's foreman.

I would rather, of course, think of your "Yes." Of beatitudes that start "Blessed are you. . ." rather than "Woe to you. . ." Of parables that comfort rather than caution.

Kierkegaard once wrote that objections to faith trace back not to doubt but "an unwillingness to obey." Pastors often preach in vain, he wrote, "because they have fought intellectually with doubt instead of fighting ethically with rebellion."

Given my almost unlimited capacity for rationalization, how do I heed a *"No, do not go that way"* when I am pretending to be deaf?

I trust, with prayer, that your 'No" will break through in time, as unmistakable as rumble tracks along the roadside.

O is for OFFER

"Who do you say that I am?"

You offer us eternal life.

"I am the resurrection and the life. Whoever believes in me, though they die, yet shall they live, and everyone who lives and believes in me shall never die." (John 11:25-26)

"For this is the will of my Father, that every one who sees the Son and who believes in him should have eternal life, and I will raise him up at the last day." (John 6:40)

I remember. . . the mother of three boys who spoke about the pain from her pancreatic cancer. Drugs provided only a thin membrane of relief, and pain squeezed through. It was the way she was dying, not death itself that grieved her. She knew death was not the end, and she spoke of heaven as though that idea was not new clothes but a garment worn for some time. When I had heard others speaking of "going to be with Jesus," the phrase seemed like self-delusion. Coming from her mouth it conveyed a possibility.

The day of her funeral, relatives and friends drove in a procession to the cemetery. Though I known her only months, she had asked that I be a pallbearer. When we lifted her casket, it proved astonishingly light. She weighed 90 pounds at the end. Her three sons stood beside the grave looking very alone in the grey afternoon.

Death did not conceal itself in these mountains. A heart attack up Dry Creek or a stroke suffered in Pineknob was felt across the valley like strands of a vibrating web.

Death on a college campus had been an anomaly; life in the coal fields was a gift. I had never lived where death so intruded. Before, it had taken old relatives and distant names. But here death took a careening swath; people I had sat beside were gone. Their absence wrenched holes in the landscape, barren as those gouged by a stripmine. Into that emptiness trickled questions about heaven that I had once found idle or archaic.

"What difference does it make?"

When did I grasp that you had come to offer us a life that does not end at death?

Your offer seems like looking into the sun. Too good to be believed. Too likely to corrupt motives. Only if I consider heaven with that approach astronomers use to see a distant star—not looking at it directly but out of the corner of the eye—do I glimpse what heaven might mean.

We search for fame and immortality in all corners of the earth so that our name might outlive our bodies. We pursue things that never were instead of something that always will be.

Your offer is right before us. If I ever needed more evidence of my fallenness this is it: I neglect the offer, distracted by the first shiny object to come along. And through the distractions, you remain still, standing before us, offering what have been seeking all our lives.

The offer of eternal life is, indeed, an offer. And, I pray, let me not turn away.

P is for PRESENCE

"Who do you say that I am?"

You promise us your presence.

"Wherever two or three are gathered, there am I among them." (Matthew 18:20)

"And when I go and prepare a place for you, I will come again and take you to myself, that when I am you may be also." (John 14:3)

"I am with you always, to the end of the age." (Matthew 28:20)

———

I remember. . . the flood at Buffalo Creek. The rains came and a high dam built carelessly from coal waste gave way. Water and mud roared downstream, funneled by a steep-walled valley, crushing lives and homes for miles.

Church members asked me to drive a van packed with boxes of warm clothing to victims. I followed crooked roads over the mountain to Buffalo Creek and found the gymnasium where survivors gathered. People huddled in blankets against walls. Children lay on cots, dozing despite the harsh lighting.

State inspectors fanned out quickly to test Coal River's own rain-swollen slag dams. No one remembered a long-abandoned underground mine whose shafts honeycombed the hillside high above the railroad tracks. Rainwater collecting in forgotten tunnels burst through the mine's plugged entrance. The ensuing mudslide uprooted trees as it swept downhill, blocking the road and bulldozing its way through one of the houses next to the railroad tracks. The family happened to be gone but arrived shortly after I did to find its home destroyed. As I watched the family survey the damage, I wondered how much more was going to happen in these valleys with their shadow of death. Our lives and their house seemed equally substantial.

What difference does it make?"

The promise is one of your presence not our security. Most of us would exchange that for insurance against sudden crushing afflictions that blindside.

But no such guarantee is given. We leave home and return to find a mudslide thrust through living room walls. We look for safety and things crumple.

No ground, save one, is sure. *"If I take the wings of the morning and dwell in the uttermost parts of the sea, even there thy hand shall lead me, and thy right hand shall hold me."* (Psalm 139:9-10)

Once I knew that only by hearsay. I still do not rely on the promise of your presence to the extent others do. But I do not doubt it. I lean in trust each day. What I once heard rumored, I feel first hand.

I write that now so that I will remember. Not that there will be no failure, loss or death, but beyond those places you will dry every tear.

Q is for QUENCH

"Who do you say that I am?"

You quench our spiritual thirst.

"If anyone thirsts, let him come to me and drink."
(John 7:37)

". . . whoever believes in me shall never thirst."
(John 6:35)

*"But whoever drinks of the water that I will give them
will never be thirsty again. The water that I will give
them will become in them a spring of water welling up
to eternal life."* (John 4:14)

I remember. . . returning to Appalachia a decade later, after
joblessness and emigration had taken a toll, and chronicling
where some people had put their trust.

In coal mines: most were no longer operating.

In education: the high school had burned and closed, its
students now bused to a neighboring county.

In churches: two of the three where the youth groups met
had been shuttered.

In the land: mountain tops had continued to be torn open
for coal, their watersheds running red from sulphur.

And for those who trusted in personal renown, it was
sobering to see even tombstones overgrown.

"What difference does it make?"

We look everywhere for something where we can place our trust.

Each day we rediscover that what we long for apart from you ultimately disappoints. "Our hearts are restless until they rest in thee," concluded St. Augustine.

Mother Teresa of Calcutta would meet religious seekers from the West who had traveled to India "looking for something." She did not speak to them of inadequacies of other faiths but asked simply, "Isn't Jesus enough for you?"

"Isn't Jesus enough?"

I answer now, "Yes." Like a well of water to drink from forever.

I have denied you in different ways over the years. Initially by evasion. Later by indifference. Now by inattention. We drink, are quenched, only to wander into afternoon heat of distractions.

Give us this day our daily bread. . . and water.

R is for RESCUE

"Who do you say that I am?"

You rescue us.

"The Son of Man came to seek and save that which was lost." (Luke 19:10)

"For God sent the Son into the world, not to condemn the world, but that the world might be saved through him." (John 3:17)

I remember. . . I nearly drowned in the river, along with the teenage son of a family who housed me. One cold spring day when rains had swollen Coal River to near flood levels, we inflated the rubber pontoons of a raft I owned and pushed off from shore. I owned only one life preserver; I urged him to wear it, he insisted that I do, and neither of us did. The current shot us downstream. For the first miles we exulted in the speed, passing forest and shacks in a blur. Belatedly we remembered a series of rapids ahead that needed to be reconnoitered, and we began to paddle toward the land. But the current had locked us in its grasp. Despite increasingly desperate paddling, we couldn't reach shore. At one point the river curled in a wide bend, pushing our raft close to a thicket of brush. With a lunge we grasped bushes, stripping leaves from branches as we yanked ourselves to land. I cut my knee on a rock as we dragged the raft to shore and stood shaking from adrenalin.

For a few minutes we watched the waves in silence. Then, with an astonishing disregard for reality, we turned and asked each other if we should keep going. Despite oncoming rapids, the current's iron hold, and blood spilling down my leg, we might well have continued. But just then the sky began to darken, raindrops fell, and the river seemed to take on a more ominous rumble. We heard no voice, but clouds increased and wind whipped the waves.

We turned from the river, folded the raft and hobbled away. On the drive home, as heavy rain fell, we each credited the other for the decision not to put the raft back in the uncontrollable river. Only later would I admit that neither of us had much to do with it.

"What difference does it make?"

Most people can tell a story of rescue. For some, from a river. For others, rescue from alcohol, accident, sickness, or despair. No shortage of perils exist.

And for some, it is rescue from certainty they do not need rescuing. Like exhausted swimmers pulled repeatedly from surf, they had imagined themselves in the retelling of the story as the lifeguard.

John Newton, long after writing, "Amazing Grace," confessed: 'My memory is nearly gone, but I remember two things: that I am a great sinner and Christ is a great Savior."

Is there a more powerful theme than 'rescue' in all the world's stories? And is there a more powerful rescuer than you?

Thank you.

S is for SPEAK

"Who do you say that I am?"

You speak as no one had before.

"Very truly, I tell you, before Abraham was, I am."
(John 8:58)

"I am the resurrection and the life. Those who believe in me, even though they die, will live, and everyone who lives and believes in me will never die. Do you believe this?" (John 11:25-26)

"No one ever spoke like this man." (John 7:46)

I remember. . . . a pastor handing me one of the leather-bound Bibles that lined the shelves of the church. I would not have pulled it down on my own, but this came more as a gift. Never underestimating my ignorance, he mentioned the edition came printed "with Jesus' words in red" to distinguish them from surrounding text. I was already familiar with the Bible. I knew the Hebrew Scriptures and the Apocrypha. I had written college papers on the Prophets. I owned a bookclub edition of the Bible and occasionally opened it randomly, reading the first verses glimpsed. But such random openings had always intentionally excluded the New Testament. I assumed I knew about it by a kind of societal osmosis.

With this gift, however, I found myself beginning to open the Bible to the Gospels, and letting my eyes fall on the red-lettered words. From church services attended as a young child I had a brushing acquaintance with some of the stories. It did not take me long to realize that I had been discounting the man who said the words before actually reading what he had said.

"What difference does it make?"

Your words imprint themselves in the pages of Scripture like photographic prints that become more distinct year by year.

I have memorized many of the verses. They are the written equivalent of checking a compass. Not that I don't lose my way.

When we realize you are who you say you are, how can we not heed your words?

I was spared the uncertainty that your words aren't recorded reliably. For me, their authenticity—and the care with which they were handed down through the generations—were never in doubt. Rather, I had simply declined to read them in the first place.

The only uncertainty is how I am going to respond to them today.

T is for TEACH

"Who do you say that I am?"

You teach us how to pray.

"This is how you should pray, 'Our Father, who art in heaven, hallowed be thy name. Thy kingdom come, thy will be done, on earth as it is in heaven. Give us this day our daily bread, and forgive us our trespasses as we forgive those who trespass against us. And lead us not into temptation, but deliver us from evil. For thine is the kingdom, the power and the glory.'"
(Matthew 6:9-13)

I remember. . . attending Sunday morning services at three churches separated by ten miles. I would begin at Dry Creek for the early service, then follow the highway along the river down to Montcoal for the 10 am service, and arrive late for the 11 am service in the small sanctuary far up the winding hollow of Pineknob.

Employed by all three congregations, I felt an obligation to put in an appearance at each one and announce upcoming activities of their sons and daughters in the various youth groups.

But before each weekly service ended, I could not help but hear the prayer that began, "Our Father, who art in heaven. . ." On any given Sunday, I found myself saying the prayer more often than I had during the preceding decade of my life.

"What difference does it make?"

I need never be at a loss for words. I know how to begin to pray. *"Our Father. . ."*

I can't take for granted the proximity invited by this prayer. Warnings against such presumption are clear: *". . .this people drawing near to me with their mouth, and honoring me with their lips, but their heart is far from me."* (Isaiah 29:13)

But we can be confident this is how you mean us to pray. Simply. Without complexity or distance.

I end each day with this prayer, said silently before sleep. When it becomes too rote, or cluttered with distractions, what brings me back to attention is recalling that I'm saying it to someone, and distractions quiet down.

And I begin again.

U is for UNITE

"Who do you say that I am?"

You unite us to each other.

"Now you are the body of Christ and individually members of it." (1st Corinthians 12:27)

"And he died for all. . ." (2nd Corinthians 5:14)

"Everyone who calls on the name of the Lord will be saved." (Romans 10:13)

I remember. . . heads bowing on Sunday mornings. I would sit in a back pew at Montcoal or Pineknob or Dry Creek as the congregation began to pray aloud:

"Our Father who art in heaven. . ."

Not "<u>My</u> Father" but "<u>Our</u> Father."

That preface linked me to the disparate individuals in the pews. I recall their faces, their oddities, as we uttered the same prayer at nearly the same pace. (One man's sepulchral bass voice invariably lagged a half sentence behind.)

For that brief moment, despite all that separated us, we admitted aloud to kinship.

"What difference does this make?"

It has come to change the way I look at others.

The first word of the Lord's Prayer draws me past boundary lines into a different country.

It underpins John Donne's assertion that "No man is an island, entire of itself/ Every man is a piece of the continent. . ." The Quaker George Fox sought "to walk cheerfully over the world, answering that of God in everyone."

My understanding of this unity is always too fleeting. A hundred things daily erode a sense of linkage to others.

Each night I begin with what the day's events have caused me to neglect.

"Our Father. . ."

V is for VANQUISHED

"Who do you say that I am?"

You vanquished death.

"The Son of Man must suffer many things and be rejected by the elders and the chief priests and the scribes and be killed, and after three days rise again." (Mark 8:31)

"But God raised him up, having loosed the pangs of death, because it was not possible for him to be held by it." (Acts 2:24)

I remember. . . the youth group practicing a musical play depicting events in Jerusalem leading up to the Crucifixion. As the final bars of music ended, church lights dimmed on the central actor, his arms outstretched as though nailed to a cross. The play ended in darkness.

In the stillness one of the teenage girls spoke: "There isn't a resurrection scene. The play ends with Jesus dead on the cross."

It was the first time I had noticed. "Well, resurrection isn't in the play," I answered. "The playwrights provided no music for it." I assumed my explanation of artistic intent should settle matters.

"But that's not the end of the story," the girl continued.

Amending the play discomforted me, but others in the youth group urged the addition. One boy living nearby left and brought back a small ultraviolet light. In minutes they improvised a scene. Now the actor portraying Jesus emerged from darkness, the light turning his white sheet florescent. In silence he walked slowly down the aisle, keeping us in his gaze. The effect was electrifying. As the numinous form passed by, the youth group gasped. So did entire congregations later that summer when the play was performed in churches through the valley.

It wasn't a sermon or a hymn, not one of highway billboards that exclaimed in oversized letters "JESUS LIVES" that finally eroded my indifference to the Resurrection. Improbably, it was a teenage girl's prodding: "But that's not the end of the story. . ."

"What difference does it make?"

Who else besides you vanquished death? We say with the disciples, *"To whom should we go? You have the words of eternal life."* (John 6:68)

To a friend who wanted to start a new religion that 'improved' upon Christianity, Talleyrand is said to have replied: "It is indeed difficult to found a new religion, but still there is one plan which you might at least try. I should recommend you to be crucified and to rise again on the third day."

As one writer noted, if your death made possible a permanent cure for sin, your resurrection made possible a permanent cure for death.

Because of what you have done, John Donne's verse— "And death shall be no more; death, thou shalt die"—becomes for each of us not empty bravado but iridescent hope.

W is for WARN

"Who do you say that I am?"

You warn us.

"Fear him who has the power to cast into hell."
(Luke 12:5)

"Then he will say to those on his left, 'Depart from me, you who are cursed, into the eternal fire prepared for the devil and his angels. For I was hungry and you gave me nothing to eat, I was thirsty and you gave me nothing to drink, I was a stranger and you did not invite me in, I needed clothes and you did not clothe me, I was sick and in prison and you did not look after me." (Matthew 25:41-43)

"Not every one that says, 'Lord, Lord,' shall enter into the kingdom of heaven, but he who does the will of my Father who is in heaven." (Matthew 7:21)

I remember. . . visiting the pastor of a neighboring parish and over dinner asking him whether he believed in a place as vindictive as hell. Unperturbed by my accusatory tone, he answered carefully. If I meant hell as a torture chamber with victims writhing in torment, then, no, he did not believe in that. He believed that hell was "separation from God." That by our choices on earth we could in the afterlife eternally distance ourselves from God's presence.

And that prospect—"the eternal loss of God"—was enough to terrify him.

Dantesque depictions of hell had long repelled me. But over dinner that evening, the pastor seeded my mind with an unconsidered image, more akin to banishment than punishment. It was a portrait of hell less visually grotesque but somehow terrifyingly equitable: those who sought eternal distance from God could receive their wish.

"What difference does it make?"

What difference? Not enough; I avoid thinking about your warnings as much as possible.

One atheist used hell to justify his disbelief: "There is one very serious defect to my mind in Christ's moral character, and that is He believed in hell." Overlooked was the possibility that hell could exist, in which case sounding a warning would not be amiss.

You told the disciples in so many words: 'On that path there are consequences for this world and the next.' Warnings conveyed not to condemn but to awaken.

Whether the risk entails fire and brimstone (as some preachers deep in the hills insisted) or endless anguish and regret, peril exists.

In the clarity of day, I am grateful to be warned. Everything we do in life has consequences. Why should we assume our relationship with you is exempt?

X is for X-RAY

"Who do you say that I am?"

You see through us.

"Jesus knew all men and needed no one to bear witness of man; for he himself knew what was in each person." (John 2:25)

"Many of the Samaritans from that town believed in him because of the woman's testimony, 'He told me everything I ever did.'" (John 4:39)

I remember. . . neighbors rocking on their front porches, alert to every passing car or ringing phone, who missed nothing. News and gossip traveled instantaneously up and down the hollows disclosing each squabble or scandal.

Everyone was visible. The valley afforded little privacy and no anonymity. Few things done remained unseen. Sins flared as conspicuously as maples in the fall.

If actions along a forested river valley were so unconcealed, few residents doubted their own lives were not transparent to God.

"What difference does it make?"

This is beyond you knowing us 'by name.'

This is deeper than a sense of your presence.

It means I cannot hide.

Body, mind, soul are visible.

Parishioners in some churches confirm the same when they say in unison: "Almighty God, to Whom all hearts are open, all desires known, and from Whom no secrets are hidden."

Few prayers seem to express so clearly a flight into reality. `

Our actions, thoughts, prayers are diagnosable by you, the Great Physician. We listen daily for the cure.

"You have searched me, Lord, and you know me." (Psalm 139:1)

You see me not as who I imagine myself to be but as who I am.

I should tremble.

Y is for YES

"Who do you say that I am?"

You say, "Yes, go this way. . ."

"Love your enemies. . . " (Matthew 5:44)

"Take up your cross. . ." (Matthew 16:24)

"Feed my sheep. . ." (John 21:17)

"You shall love the Lord your God with all your heart, and with all your soul, and with all your mind, and with all your strength. . . and you shall love your neighbor as yourself." (Mark 12:30-31)

I remember . . . in late spring the youth group painting the Pineknob home of a widow. The teenagers balanced on high ladders, nimbly painting under eaves, conversing through an open window with the woman's sick young son.

Isolated incidents—a callous remark by a pastor, violated vows by a priest, embezzled funds by a church treasurer—can outweigh a century of Christian charity; an experience with a single hypocrite eclipses histories of a dozen martyrs.

But at times the converse proves true: a single glimpsed episode—the caring for a widow's house, the feeding of a stranger—can mute the howling of inquisitors and crusaders.

I once judged Christianity by the behavior of its believers and found it wanting. In West Virginia by the same standard I found it inviting. I would come to realize more slowly that, thankfully, Christianity hinged on something more reliable than Christians.

"What difference does it make?"

Your words direct me into corners of the world I would not visit otherwise. To look people in the eye who I might have turned away from before.

Ignatius Loyola asked himself three questions that prod our own consciences: "What have I done for Christ? What am I doing for Christ? What should I be doing for Christ?"

I think the hallmark of joy is someone knowing how you would have them live, and hoping they are doing your work, and praying that at the evening of life they might live with you. They see with their eyes this world, while hearing with their ears, mindful as deer in the forest, the approach of the next.

"*Follow me*," you said, in a succinct definition of discipleship.

And it is we who respond, "Yes."

Z is for the END

"Who do you say that I am?"

You are our beginning and our end.

"I am the Alpha and the Omega, the First and the Last, the Beginning and the End." (Revelation 22:13)

"In my Father's house are many mansions: if it were not so, I would have told you. I go to prepare a place for you. And if I go and prepare a place for you, I will come again, and receive you unto myself; that where I am, there you may be also." (John 14: 2-3)

"For this is the will of my Father, that everyone who looks on the Son and believes in him should have eternal life, and I will raise them up on the last day." (John 6:40)

I remember. . . my last day in the valley. As I drove away over the final ridge, I pulled to the side of the road and peered back into the watershed. Smoke from chimneys drifted up from green ravines. I could still hear the river through the canopy of trees. For a moment I wanted to linger, to postpone my departure, as though the year could not travel with me.

Asked what they had given me that year, most residents along Coal River would have answered 'an invitation'—to homes, meals, weddings, funerals. I took with gratitude what they each offered. But few would have presumed to single out their most enduring invitation.

"What difference does it make?"

Each of us has a place where we begin to listen for the first time.

In following years I would return often to West Virginia to see the valley and feel its rain, to retrieve strands that wound into a rope of faith, and to heed again from that setting what you have given us.

I have denied you in various ways over the years, now most often by failing to remember, my attention evanescent as a wisp of mist. But as no shortage of witnesses along the river could testify, though we may forsake, we are never forsaken. *"I will not leave you comfortless; I will come to you."* (John 14:18)

We are not given unlimited days. *"For now we see through a glass darkly; but then face to face: now I know in part; but then shall I know even as also I am known."*(1st Corinthians 13:12)

I do not know what my dying will bring. But I am hopeful of who.

You who have known us from the beginning.

DAVID DOUGLAS works with non-profit organizations that improve access to clean drinking water inter-nationally and that advocate for increased U.S. foreign aid for health and development. He has written for Protestant and Catholic publications and is the author of *Wilderness Sojourn: Notes in the Desert Silence* and co-author with his wife, Deborah, of *Pilgrims in the Kingdom: Travels in Christian Britain*. He and Deborah live in Santa Fe, New Mexico, and are the parents of two grown children, Katie and Emily.